let dreams come true

An Advent course

Ray Simpson

kevin
mayhew

First published in 2005 by
KEVIN MAYHEW LTD
Buxhall, Stowmarket, Suffolk, IP14 3BW
E-mail: info@kevinmayhewltd.com
www.kevinmayhewltd.com

9 8 7 6 5 4 3 2 1 0

ISBN 184417 423 9
Catalogue No. 1500814

Cover painting by Angela Palfrey
Cover design by Angela Selfe
Edited by Marian Reid
Typeset by Richard Weaver

This course is suitable for established groups and cells, and for groups specially convened to meet during the November/December season. Individuals may also profit from it if they omit the ice-breakers and use the group discussion material for personal reflection.

Groups may use any or all of the eight weekly sessions. A good time to start if all eight sessions are used is the first week of November, which, with good reason, used to mark the beginning of the year. If the group meets only in Advent, the four weeks before Christmas, it is best to start with Week 5. It is envisaged that each weekly session should be about an hour to ninety minutes long.

The units follow this format with some variations:

Bring
Music
Icebreaker
Candle lighting
Bible reading
Meditation
Groups
Response
Devotion (silence, prayer, singing)
Take away (actions, lessons, inspirations)

Devotional material during candle lighting is taken from Volume 1 of *The Celtic Prayer Book, Prayer Rhythms*; Volume 2, *Saints of the Isles*; Volume 3, *Healing the Land*; and Volume 4, *Great Celtic Christians*. Some suggestions for music are made in the text. The CD *Margaret Rizza: Her Music for Advent and Christmas* (Kevin Mayhew Ltd) provides music that is suitable for any of the sessions. During meditations it helps to sit upright, breathing rhythmically, with feet flat on the floor and palms resting upwards on the thighs. Keep plenty of pauses.

About the author

Ray Simpson is a co-founder of the worldwide Community of Aidan and Hilda and is its first guardian. He is a priest and pastor in the Christian Church, and a well-known author. He lives on The Holy Island of Lindisfarne, near to the Community's Retreat and Guest House, The Open Gate, Holy Island, Berwick Upon Tweed, TD15 2SD, UK.

Also by Ray Simpson:

Celtic Daily Light: a spiritual journey throughout the year
Church of the Isles: a prophetic strategy for renewal
Exploring Celtic Spirituality: historic roots for our future
A Pilgrim Way: a new Celtic monasticism for everyday people
Prayer Rhythms for Busy People: a pocket companion

The Celtic Prayer Book is published in four volumes:

Volume One
Prayer Rhythms: fourfold patterns for each day and season

Volume Two
Saints of the Isles: a year of feasts

Volume Three
Healing the Land: natural seasons, sacraments and special services

Volume Four
Great Celtic Christians: alternative worship

Contents

Introduction

Seasons

We have seasons for football and fashion – so why not for faith development? Early British people kept three seasons free for the pursuit of spiritual development. These they called the 'three Lents'. The second 'Lent' is the period before Christmas. Churches now call this 'Advent'.

In the English language we speak about the 'advent' of a significant event or person – usually this advent happens after a period of build-up and anticipation.

Ancient Jews were typical of many peoples. They had beliefs, dreams and hopes, but these were constantly dashed on the rocks of human selfishness. So they began to believe in the advent of a leader. This leader would somehow resolve the dilemma that human hopes are destroyed by human selfishness. Jesus – many people of all religions and nationalities believe – actually did emerge as this leader, a leader for all peoples, one who could outlive the worst that humans could do to him.

The advent of this leader is celebrated year by year by giving Jesus an 'official' birthday that coincides, in the northern hemisphere, with the darkest depths of winter. In the four weeks before Christmas ways of building up anticipation and of preparing to receive 'the God who comes' are explored. This cycle is something to be lived inside ourselves and expressed through visual corporate acts.

Advent is preceded by another season. Samhain (pronounced Soween), which begins on 1 November, marked the start of the year in ancient Britain and Ireland. The seventh-century Northumbrian historian Bede informs us that the Saxon (i.e., early English) word for November means 'blood month', because of all the blood from slaughtered animals. In November the cattle which could not pasture on the outlying places in winter had to be slaughtered. The bonfires we associate with this time of year get their name from the bone fires in which the inedible parts of the carcases were burned.

The November fires are also associated with the idea of clearing the decks for winter; the leaves and the excess things of summer are swept up and burned. Something in the human psyche, too, needs to clear the decks, to accept a reduction in the number of choices that are available to us, and to settle down. Only then are we free to walk towards the gate that leads out of this world into the next.

This is a season that draws our attention to different forms of dying not only because cattle were slaughtered, but also because animals and humans alike are more prone to cold, sickness, hunger and death.

In pre-Christian Celtic myth, on Samhain night the gates of the Other World were open, allowing communion with the ancestors. The Christian celebration of all those who have passed into heaven, All Saints, makes this a reality for us. November is a time of remembrance: we remember our ancestors and recent loved ones who have died, the war dead, and great saints of God.

In pre-Christian times this was also seen as a time of change and transformation where both the past and present met with the uncertain tides of the future yet to come. Druids and bards would forecast coming patterns of farming and hunting, eclipses of the sun, storms, and warfare. It is a good time for Christians to become aware of the dreams God is putting into our souls. So the first four units of this week explore the themes of the November season.

Have a go

Each Advent an intrepid group of people walk the pilgrim way across the low-tide sands to the Holy Island of Lindisfarne, on England's north-east coast. This walk can be wet and windy.

One year, two plump ladies fresh from sunny Australia agreed to join the two-and-a-half-mile Advent Prayer Walk. They started out, even though there was a freezing gale. One of the ladies was nearly blown backwards. She became so exhausted that she clung to each pilgrim post for what seemed an eternity, before walking backwards to the next post and the next wait.

The walk took three times longer than usual. I thought to myself 'What a waste of time. It's too cold to pray.' Some weeks later, however, I received a photograph from the two ladies. On it they had written: 'the most memorable day of our lives'.

They had a go at that Advent 'course' and found it memorable. We, too, can have a go at this Advent Course and find it memorable.

> O Christ, Son of the living God,
> may your holy angels guard our journey.
> May they watch over us as we meet,
> and hover around our beds as we sleep.
> Let them reveal to us in our dreams
> visions of your glorious truth.

Listen to the Dark

BRING

The leader brings: a candle to light; music; a seed to give to each person.

ICEBREAKER

Each person goes up to ten others and says: 'Did you know that in ancient times in Western climes the new year began on 1 November? Can you guess why that was?'

CANDLE LIGHTING

Light one candle and switch off or dim the lights.

Leader   In the darkness we can see the splendour
of the universe –
blankets of stars,
the solitary glowings of the planets.

All   Come, O God Most High.

Leader   In the darkness of the womb
mortals are nurtured
and the Christ-child was made ready for the
journey into light.

All   Come, O God Most High.

Leader   In the darkness the wise three found the star
that led them to you.

All   Come, O God Most High.

Leader   In the darkness of dreams you spoke to Joseph
and the wise ones.

All	Come, O God Most High.
Leader	In the darkness of despair and distress we watch for a sign of hope from the Light of Lights.
All	Come, O God Most High.

(*Prayer Rhythms* Advent Night Prayer)

BIBLE READING   Isaiah 45:1-4

In this passage the prophet Isaiah speaks to Cyrus, the emperor of the Persian Empire around 530 BC. Isaiah's people, Israel, had been conquered and exiled to the capital city of this empire, Babylon. But the new emperor, Cyrus, was willing to respect different cultures, and even to restore religious institutions such as the Jews' temple (2 Chronicles 36:22-23). Although such places may have seemed to him dark, far away corners of his empire, they contained treasures, Isaiah suggests, waiting to be discovered.

Now read the passage. The leader may give other teaching about this passage, or the group may immediately take three minutes to silently reflect upon a) what were some treasures of the darkness that Isaiah might have had in mind? b) what are some treasures of darkness for us?

GROUPS

Share, for a few minutes, these treasures of darkness in twos or small groups.

MUSIC

There may be singing or listening to music, for example Vivaldi's *Four Seasons*.

MEDITATION

This is the time of year when the cold and the dark seem set to take over, a time when our instinct is to withdraw. Our ego resists the idea of accepting limits, so we may disguise our feelings by going on seasonal shopping sprees or binges. Yet think of the animals who frolic in spring but hibernate in winter. Think of the wonders of spring flowers – they would not be able to burst forth if they had not first been buried in the wintry earth.

A human life begins not on the day of birth, but on the day of conception, and the encroaching mists and dark of this time are like a wintry womb, a period of protected gestation, disengaged from the long, light days of heavy duty. So it is a time of transition: a time both of ending and beginning.

So how should a Christian respond to this time of year? By embracing the God-given rhythm of the season, and going with the flow of the ebb tide. November's grey days, dark nights, cold rains and thick fog help us to accept that we are mortal. They invite us to spend less time dashing around, purchasing things, starting schemes. They invite us to take more time for the inner life, for study, to be alone and still with God.

Think now of these dark days as a wintry womb. In the darkness of the womb mortals are nurtured and the Christ-child was made ready for his journey into light. Before that, as the Eternal Light, he had to make ready to enter this dark womb. Are we, who are made to reflect divine attributes, ready to enter into 'the winter womb'?

To be ready, we must become like a seed. We must be stripped of pretensions to be self-made. We must be content to be formed silently, slowly, and not rush here and there.

Blessed is a womb. A necessary place. A place of shelter. A place of formation. A place free from predators, distractions and enticing but life-threatening pursuits.

Let us relax, breathe deeply, and in our minds enter winter's womb with Christ accompanying us.

Spend a few minutes using your imagination to visualise what happens.

There may be a sharing of these visualisations.

DEVOTION

There may be singing (for example, 'Lead kindly Light'), music, or spontaneous prayers.

Leader   Stripped of inessentials we stand, rooted in you.
We place into your hands winter's patterns
which you call us now to live
in the stillness of the bare earth.
We invite you to do your work in us.

All   At the drawing in of the year may our
contemplations bring us peace.
May the soft mists of God's presence wrap
us in their gentle folds.
And in the darkness may we find true light.

TAKE AWAY

A seed. Place this in a prominent place at home to remind you to live like a seed in winter's earth, allowing God to work mysteriously in you.

Listen to the Deep

BRING

The leader brings: a candle to light; music; sheets of blank paper and pen or pencils.

MUSIC

Sibelius's *Finlandia,* or something similar.

ICEBREAKER

Each person asks up to ten others: 'What do people mean when they ask "Are you in touch with your shadow?"'.

CANDLE LIGHTING

A candle is lit.

Leader   At this time of year there are many shadows.
There is an aspect of ourselves that has been named
The Shadow. The Shadow consists of parts of us that
we bury because we think they are unacceptable.
When we consciously bury something we call it
suppression. When we unconsciously bury something
we call it repression. This can produce depression.

Reader   Your presence supports us through
the dark night, so we may hail
the coming source of Light.

All   Hail, gladdening Light of God's
pure glory poured.
Holiest of holies, Jesus Christ our Lord.

Reader   Jesus Christ, the light of the world.

All	Christ in life's deep shadows.
	Christ in shades of death,
	Christ in mists of memory.
	Christ in wintry earth.
Reader	As we linger with the shades of memory . . .
All	Recall us to your Presence, touch us with your hope.
Reader	Our beginning and our end
	are by your command, O God.
All	Before mortals were born
	they were known and loved by you.
	They have their worth eternally in you.

BIBLE READING   Psalm 42

This prayer-poem was recorded by someone who was in deep waters. It brings out before God memories that might otherwise have remained buried. It clothes with words some of the deep aches of our own souls. As it is read, note a phrase that resonates most deeply with you.

Psalm 42 is read aloud by one or more readers.

Any who wish may repeat the phrase in this psalm that resonated deeply with them.

MEDITATION

Memory is a beautiful and God-given faculty of the soul. Computers can store information, but they have no soul memory. Soul memory is nourishment. It is a way to make meaning out of what otherwise might be a meaningless collection of data.

But memory can be thrown away or lost. The Irish poet John O'Donohue has said: 'There never was a day which did not get buried in the graveyard of the night.' If we turn our 'night' seasons into frenzied day, memory remains a buried treasure.

God holds everything that has happened to us and in us in his heart. Memory is a way to touch what God holds in his heart for us. Let us take time, in this month of remembrance, to draw living water from the wells of our memory.

EXERCISE

Draw a 'Life Line'. Draw a straight line across a blank sheet of paper. Mark sections such as: infant/junior/teenager/starting work/ starting a home/focal relationships/losses/discoveries. Note down a memory from each period that was formative in your life.

SHARING IN TWOS

Share any memory that you feel comfortable about revealing.

DEVOTION

Words that evoke awareness of God's love are quietly sung or listened to on a recording, for example, Margaret Rizza's 'Sanctum'.

Reader   God give you grace to see
into the beauty buried in your soul.
God give you courage to journey
into the pain buried in your soul.
God give you wisdom to gather
the fragments of memory.
God help you to embrace the hidden parts
until they become part of the whole.

TAKE AWAY

A memory that has come to the forefront of your awareness.

Leader   Remind the group to bring a photograph or memento of a deceased person who means a lot to them to the next session.

Listen to Death

BRING

A photograph or memento, if you wish, of a deceased person who means a lot to you.

The leader brings a candle to light; requiem music; a standing cross; night lights to place on a table.

ICEBREAKER

Each person asks about five others: ' "Remember, remember the fifth of November." What do you remember about it?'

CANDLE LIGHTING

Leader   This season draws our attention to different forms of dying, not only because cattle are slaughtered, but also because the earth lies bare and cold. Accompanied by the frantic lowing of doomed beasts, people contemplated the tragedies that might await them, and became acutely aware, and perhaps frightened, of their own mortality. They also thought about those who had died before them, and sought to learn from them.

This is the season of remembering our ancestors. It is also the season of remembering all souls, simply because every soul leaves an imprint on the landscape. But tonight we especially focus on great souls who were close to God and whose example or words we do well to remember.

We light a candle in their memory.

A candle is lit

Reader	We remember before you, Immortal God:
First	Our fathers and mothers and theirs.
Second	Those we were closely bound to, and those more distant who touched us through them.
Third	Friends and relations.
Fourth	Those who served you faithfully in their life.
Fifth	Those who hurt or harmed us.
Sixth	Those who suffered an untimely death.
Seventh	Those whose faith is known to you alone.
Eighth	Brothers and sisters in Christ.
Ninth	Those who inspire us through their lives, their writings, their deeds of love.
Tenth	Holy and healing souls.
All	They are yours, O Lord, you lover of souls.

There may be singing

BIBLE READING Genesis 28:10-16; John 1:47-51

This is a 'thin' season, that is, the gap between this world and the next seems to be thin, so our forebears come to mind. These may be ancestors by blood or people with whom we feel a spiritual affinity.

Jacob's grandfather, Abraham was dead, but he without doubt treasured in his heart the promise God had given to Abraham, which Abraham had passed on to his grandchildren. In this dream, the promise is also given to Jacob. Later, Jacob's name is changed to Israel.

In John 1:47-51 Jesus says that a man of integrity named Nathaniel is a son of Israel (i.e. Jacob). There is no suggestion he was related by blood. So in what sense was he a son of Israel?

The idea seems to be that we can be spiritual sons and daughters of God-guided personalities, if we listen to their God-inspired words and become in tune with them.

What else do you learn from these two passages? Discuss.

MEDITATION

The following story beautifully links one of our ancient myths with the Bible and our Christian faith. Dunadd is the hill of rock, near Kilmartin in Kintyre, which is a natural fortification and the most ancient seat of any British king. If you visit it, you will see carvings of a basin and a boar and two footprints which go back to the time of the Picts.

Tradition has it that the bare footprint was made by Fergus, when he was crowned the first king of the Irish colony of Dalriada in AD 500. He brought with him, moreover, a very special and sacred stone. It was the stone which Jacob used as his pillow when he dreamed of a ladder that reached from earth to heaven, and on which angels went up and down. It became known as the stone of destiny. It was here that St Columba anointed and crowned Aidan as King of Dalriada shortly after he came to Iona, which some identify as the prototype of the coronation of British monarchs that continues to this day. This stone of destiny was taken by the conquering English to Westminster Abbey, and was returned to Scotland for the start of the third millennium.

The modern discovery of DNA tends to reinforce the wisdom of primal peoples in making spaces to focus on their ancestors, because, like it or not, for better or worse, we carry our ancestors in us and they have contributed to us.

Meister Eckhart, when asked where a person's soul goes when they die, replied: 'No place.' John O'Donohue points out in his book, *Anamcara*, that we have falsely driven the eternal out into some distant galaxy in our mind's eye, yet the eternal world is not a different place but a different state of being. He recounts how an Irishman asked his priest, 'Where are the dead?' and the priest said he was not to ask questions like that. But the man persisted, so the priest raised his right hand. The man looked out under the raised right arm and saw the souls of the departed everywhere around, as thick as the dew on blades of grass.

If there is time, someone might volunteer to tell a story of an ancestor. This is a good time to get out photograph albums and family trees and to tell stories of those who have gone before.

21

What if you are not very proud of your ancestors – what if there are skeletons in the cupboard? Ask yourself: 'What pain have they to tell me of? What mistakes should I avoid?' And invite Jesus, the mediator between earth and heaven, to put into your hearts the right replies.

Remembrance of the dead is given importance in the Sayings of the Desert Christians, who urged: If there are graves in the area where you live, go to them constantly, and meditate on those lying there . . . and when you hear that a brother or sister is about to leave this world to go to the Lord, go and stay with them in order to contemplate how a soul leaves the body.

DEVOTION & MUSIC

God has put within us a need to recollect, from time to time, those people who, though now dead, have loved or influenced us in person or through their sayings or writings: to remember them, to savour them, to talk to God about them, and perhaps to complete a grieving process. Why not remember these in a few moments of silence today? Thank God for them, and keep them in mind throughout the week.

A well-known piece of requiem music is played

During the music, think of someone you knew or have heard or read about whose example or words mean a lot to you. When you are ready, light a night-light in their memory, and place it by the cross on the table. After all have done this, and after a further short silence, the leader says:

Leader   Since it was you, O Christ, who bought each
soul – at the time it gave up its life, at the time
of returning to clay, at the time of shedding of
blood, at the time of severing of the breath, at
the time you delivered judgement – may your
peace be on your ingathering of souls.

22

Jesus Christ, son of gentle Mary, your peace
be upon your own ingathering.

(*Echoes a prayer in the* Carmina Gadelica)

All We will go forward with the fire of Christ
re-kindled by the memory of those who have
gone before us. Amen.

TAKE AWAY

Think of a memory of a dead person whose example or words inspire you.

Make a note to record significant dreams, and bring this next week if you have any.

WEEK 4
Listen to Dreams

BRING

Anything you have noted down about a dream that seems significant to you. This could be your own or a dream from the Bible, or that of a famous person, or from a film or book.

The leader brings a picture or projection of a rood screen or of the Haiti Tree of Life.

ICEBREAKER

Ask any three people: 'Can you tell me a dream that you think is important?' If they say, 'Yes', listen to them tell it.

CANDLE LIGHTING

Light a candle.

Candle- It is better to light one candle than to curse
lighter the darkness.
Let this candle represent a dream that God puts
into our souls.
Let this candle represent a dream of a land of
promise such as God gave to Moses.
Let this candle represent a dream of justice
restored, such as he gave Martin Luther King.

Reader I have a dream that one day on the red hills
of Georgia the children of former slaves and
the children of former slave owners will be
able to sit down together at the table of brotherhood.*

---

* From Martin Luther King's speech at a Civil Rights march in Washington, 28 August 1963.

I just want to do God's will.

And he's allowed me to go up to the mountain.

And I've looked over and I've seen the promised land.*

MUSIC

Dream music such as 'Climb Every Mountain' from *The Sound of Music.*

BIBLE READING   Matthew 3:1-10

Trees are powerful dream symbols. We will look at two Bible dreams about a tree. The first is a dream that came to John, the Forerunner of Jesus.

The message is that those who live false lives are like trees about to be cut down. Jesus made a similar point when he said that a person who hurls abuse at another human being, who is in fact their brother or sister, is liable to end up on the always-smouldering town scrap heap (Matthew 5:22).

Now we read of another tree in the dream of a prophet who lived in the same country as John the Forerunner, 650 years before him. The message, in short, is: 'I have a dream of a tree stump. Out of this stump a new shoot will grow.'

One person or all read Isaiah 10:33-11:9.

MEDITATION

Display a picture or projection of a rood screen or of the Haiti Tree of Life. A once-powerful tree becomes a mere stump. It looks as if that is the end of the tree. But from within its trunk a new growth shoots up, green and tender, straight and true, which becomes a branch.

There is a shortened genealogy that traces Jesus' family tree to Jesse, the father of King David (Matthew 1:5-16). Jesus grows out of the tree stump that was Jesse. This is a fulfilment of the prophet's dream.

---

* From Martin Luther King's speech in Memphis, 3 April 1968, the day before he was killed.

After Jesus' death and resurrection he was sometimes called 'The Tree of Life' because the two beams of wood to which Jesus was nailed were in the shape of a tree trunk with two horizontal branches; and because the wood had been cut from a tree. 1 Peter 2:24 states: 'Christ carried our sins in his own body on the tree so that we might be finished with sin and alive to all that is good.'

Now look at the picture. What speaks to you? What makes you sad? For what aspect of Christ does it make you thankful? What hopes does it spark in you?

A few minutes of silence.

GROUPS

In groups of four, share thoughts that came to you during the silence.

OPTIONAL ACTIVITY

Cut-outs of a tree may be made and each person may write on one: 'I place the tree of Christ between me and each dark thing'.

DEVOTION

When early Irish Christians were lying in bed worrying about some trouble, they would imagine the tree of Christ's cross being placed between them and the trouble. Imagine yourself lying in bed tonight. Repeat this Irish prayer slowly, line by line, after the reader:

I come to rest in the name of the Father.
Lying on my bed in your name, O noble King.
I place the tree upon which Christ was crucified
between me and the heavy nightmare
between me and each evil thing.

After a pause, sing a suitable song, e.g. 'Bread of Heaven', 'O Love that wilt not let me go' or 'The trees of the field shall clap their hands'.

27

Reader   Life-giver,

All   Bring buds to flower,
bring rain to the earth,
bring songs to our hearts.

Reader   Renewer,
may fields become green,
may beauty emerge,
may dreams come to pass.

(*Healing the Land*, Night Prayer for spring)

O God, I see your story in flowing streams,
in sporting teams, in people's dreams.
As the water in the stream makes its journey
to the sea, so I will flow with your Spirit and
your saints into you.

(Echoes Kiwi prayers in *Saints of the Isles*)

May the building stones of our lives be
re-mortared.
May our dreams be restocked with
sacred meaning.
May our journeys lead to peace.

(*Great Celtic Christians*)

This week:
sleep in peace;
sleep soundly;
sleep in love.
Weaver of dreams,
weave well in you as you sleep.

(*Healing the Land*, Night Prayer for autumn)

TAKE AWAY

Cut-outs of the tree which may be pinned to a garment.
  Keep a dream diary.

1st Week of Advent
Listen to Parents-in-God

BRING
The leader should have ready an Advent wreath with four purple or red candles and a white candle in the middle, to represent Jesus' birth.

ICEBREAKER
Each person asks up to six others: 'What's the wisest thing a parent figure from the past has said that's influenced you?'

CANDLE LIGHTING & MUSIC
Dim the lights; play or listen to an awakening rumble of drums or a bugle call.

Reader   In the wasteland may the Glory shine.
           In the land of the lost may the King make
           his home.

           Light one coloured candle

Reader   All-knowing God, poets and parents-in-God
           picture and pattern your ways.

All   Forgive us for following idols and illusions.

           Let there be a moment of silence, then turn
           the lights up

BIBLE READING
Abraham leaves behind the comfort zones that prevented him discovering what God had in store for him and for the world.

    Read Genesis 12:1-3. Then one or two people state in their own words what they think the waking, living dream that God gave to Abraham might have been.

Read Genesis 15:1-6. Abraham and his wife Sarah were past childbearing age. What five letter word beginning with T best sums up Abraham's attitude as a role model?

Abraham and Sarah had a child named Isaac. What incident with Isaac illustrates Abraham's amazing trust in God against all the odds? (Genesis 22).

TRUST is a quality which Abraham models for us: read Romans 4:16-17.

HOSPITALITY is a second quality he models for us. Read Genesis 19:1-3. The early Christians took to heart this second quality as much as the first. The following words from the letter to Hebrew Christians refer back to this episode of Abraham giving hospitality to strangers: read Hebrews 13:1-2.

All may sing a song such as 'I cannot tell'

MEDITATION

Muslims, Jews and Christians are all 'children of Abraham'. The rock on which Abraham offered a sacrifice to God is held to be the site of the Jewish Temple which is now a mosque. After visiting the Dome of the Rock I had a dream. It was of a huge version of a rotating stage such as is used in theatres. The first act was set in one third of the rotating stage, the next act in the second section, and the last act in the third section. In the dream, advanced technology enabled the first part of the rotating stage to be a mosque. The second was a temple, and the third was a church. On Fridays the 'set' was the mosque, on Saturdays it was the temple, and on Sundays it was the church.

I happened to get into a conversation with an Israeli security guard and told him this dream. To my surprise, he took this seriously, and suggested I made it public.

This dream seems impossible. But who knows if it could not come to pass? Even if it never comes to pass in a physical sense, it is rich in symbolism, and can come to fulfilment in other ways, through the friendship under God of the different children of Abraham.

What is your dream? As dream music plays, allow thoughts perhaps inspired by a spiritual parent, to come to the surface, even if they seem impossible. Write them down if you wish. After five minutes any dreams or other thoughts that came to you can be shared.

Dream music can now be played

GROUPS

Take about ten minutes to share, in threes, any dreams or thoughts that have been inspired by a spiritual parent.

DEVOTION

Leader Holy One, who raises up God-guided personalities, we thank you for Abraham and spiritual forbears who laid foundations without which the world would never have been ready for your coming.

All Thank you for the Abrahams of this world.

Leader Shaper of peoples, who through Moses gave guidance that would make a people great,

All Thank you for nation-shapers like Moses.

Leader Great God who mothers us all, who through Deborah's wise counsel held a nation together,

All Thank you for the wise women of every age.

Leader King of kings, who through King David was enthroned in the heart of your people,

All Thank you for Davids who leap and labour to enthrone you in the people's affections.

There may be singing

TAKE AWAY

An inspiration born of a spiritual parent.

31

2nd Week of Advent

Listen to Prophets
Who Proclaim God's Breakthroughs

BRING

Bibles. Sheets of paper and pencils or crayons for each person. The group should have ready an Advent wreath with four purple or red candles and a white candle in the middle, to represent Jesus' birth.

ICEBREAKER

Each person asks up to ten others: 'When I say the word "prophet", what person comes into your mind?'

CANDLE LIGHTING & MUSIC

Dim the lights.

Reader   In the wasteland may the Glory shine.
In the land of the lost may the King
make his home.
Light one coloured candle

First   We light this candle for spiritual forebears who picture and pattern your ways.

All   Forgive us for following idols and illusions.
Light a second coloured candle

Second   We light this candle:
for prophets' words which shine like candles
in the night.

Third   For people who burn with conviction and pass it on.

Fourth   For people who listen to God and tell what they hear.

Fifth	For people who give a sleeping lion its roar.
Sixth	For prophets like Isaiah, who proclaimed the coming of a Child Messiah.
All	Forgive us for hiding truth in the dark.

Listen to a recording of all or some of the first nine tracks of Handel's *Messiah* (omitting the opening overture), beginning 'Comfort ye my people' and ending with 'Kings shall come to the brightness of thy rising'.

BIBLE READING   Isaiah 9:6-7

Before we begin, remember that people like Isaiah were stirred up with a prophetic vision. They perhaps passed it on to a gathering of national leaders, or to the people in the city centre. Then it got repeated in various places. Someone wrote it down on a scroll. These scrolls were later collected together. Much later they were printed in Bibles as we now have them. We shall now read one of these prophecies. As it is read, think of the word that most strikes you.

Read the verses, then have a pause.

What word struck you in that reading? And why? Have a time of sharing.

MEDITATION & GROUPS

Our lives are so rushed, and we are inundated with so many words, sounds and images that we hardly know what we think, let alone what God thinks. Yet God never stops speaking. God never stops coming. And we are designed with a capacity to listen to God in our heart's deepest core. We will pair up with the person next to us. During three minutes of silence, think of what might be the most important thing God wants either for yourself, for your group partner, for the Church, or for our society. The leader will ring a bell after about three minutes. Then write down or draw a picture of your conviction. If you are blank, just draw any picture that comes into your mind.

After the bell is rung again, people may share in pairs, if they wish, what they have written or pictured.

DEVOTION

Leader   Let us pray.

All   Calm us to wait for the gift of Christ.
Cleanse us to prepare the way for Christ.
Teach us to contemplate the wonder of Christ.
Anoint us to bear the life of Christ.

Leader   Let us wake to Christ's summons,
urgent in our midst.

All   Let us wake to the truth that his power alone
will last.

Leader   The worlds that scorn him will vanish like a dream.

All   When he comes to his own all good will flow
as one.

*There may be singing, such as 'Open our eyes, Lord', 'Long
ago prophets knew', or 'Mine eyes have seen the glory'*

Reader   Those whose faces are turned always towards
the sun's rising
see the living light on its path approaching.

(Kathleen Raine, Lindisfarne)

Let the rumble of traffic diminish
and the song of the birds grow clear,
and may the Son of God come striding towards you,
walking on these stones.

(St Aidan's Chapel, Bradford Cathedral)

TAKE AWAY

What will you take away in your hearts this week? Any may give
their answer.

We can all take away the prayer. Give or write out copies of the
prayer: 'Calm us to wait for the gift of Christ'.

WEEK 7
3rd Week of Advent
Listen to Forerunners
Who Prepare God's Way

BRING

The group should have ready gift tags for each group member, plus an Advent wreath with four purple or red candles and a white candle in the middle, to represent Jesus' birth.

ICEBREAKER

Each person asks three or four others: 'Have you ever run through a rough, hilly or busy place? Tell me about it.'

CANDLE LIGHTING & MUSIC

During the candle lighting, quiet background music such as from the film *Chariots of Fire* may be played.

Leader	In the wasteland may the Glory shine. In the land of the lost may the King make his home.
	Light one coloured candle
First	All-knowing God, poets and parents-in-God, picture and pattern your ways.
All	Forgive us for following idols and illusions.
	Light one coloured candle
Second	All-seeing God, prophets shine like candles in the night.
All	Forgive us for staying in the dark.
	Light one coloured candle

Third	All-holy God, forerunners like John clear obstacles from your path.
All	Forgive us for blocking your way.

Listen to the music for a short while

BIBLE READING

Jesus' cousin, the hermit John, was an 'athlete of the Spirit'. He emerged from the desert to spearhead a national movement away from selfish pursuits and towards God's purposes. After a time it became clear that he was preparing the way for God to come through Jesus. Some call him John the Baptist, because he baptised Jesus in the River Jordan. Others call him John the Forerunner, because he was like a runner, clearing obstacles from the road that God would tread.

Read Luke 1:76. This was a divine prophecy given to John's father before John was born.

Read Mark 1:1-8.

Take a few minutes to discuss: 'What is the connection between Verse 3, 'Get the road ready', and Verse 4, 'Turn away from your sins'? What practical changes do you think people might have made?

Reader Luke 3:10-14.

This gives two practical examples of how people then could prepare the way for God to come. One was to get honest. Another was to be generous – to give to those more needy than ourselves. In several religions this is known as almsgiving. These remain two ways in which we today can prepare God's way.

GROUPS

In groups of three, mention examples of people today who have prepared God's way through honesty or generosity.

MEDITATION

Nicholas, a parish priest in Myra, the area of Turkey now known as Dembre, is a glorious example of such an almsgiver. Although no doubt he himself lived modestly, he had inherited money from his wealthy parents. When a parishioner who, having lost a fortune, and being unable to give his daughters a marriage dowry, planned to sell his daughters into prostitution, Nicholas secretly dropped sufficient money for a dowry down a chimney at night. This landed in a sock which had been left to dry in the fire grate.

That is the origin of the Christmas stocking, and 'St Nicklaus', who was later declared to be a saint, is the origin of Santa Claus. The proto Santa gift came from a heart filled with compassion for individuals in need.

As we reflect on John, and how we can be forerunners for God by being honest and generous, and as we reflect on Nicklaus, and how we can prepare for Christ's birth by giving thoughtful gifts, let us think, in the silence, of someone we know whom we can give a gift to. It may be that their need is not for money or food, but for thoughtfulness. Think about our Christmas giving. Choose gifts of thoughtfulness for those who most need them, gifts that come out of a heart of love. When you are ready, take one gift tag and write on it the name of the person who has come to mind in the silence, to whom you will give something, whether it is big or small, a promise, a product or a prayer.

A few minutes' silence, during which any may take and write on a gift tag

GROUPS

In groups of three, share anything from the Bible reading or meditation that has struck you, or a question you have.

DEVOTION

There may be singing, such as 'Take my life'

Leader   Holy God, holy and mighty,
who brought holy John to birth in a barren womb,
and who can bring a new thing to birth in
a barren land – bring to birth in us that new
thing that is your will.

Thank you for making John a forerunner
who prepared a way for you.

All   Help us to prepare a way for you.

Reader   Where there is falsehood,

All   Help us prepare a way for you.

Reader   Where there is violence,

All   Help us prepare a way for you.

Reader   Where there is abuse of others,

All   Help us prepare a way for you.

Reader   Where there is meanness,

All   Help us prepare a way for you.

*Form a circle. Each one places their gift tag
in front of them*

All   Generous God, circle these whom you have
put on our hearts this day.
Keep cold without, keep warmth within.
Keep hate without, keep love within.
Keep meanness without,
keep generosity within. Amen.

TAKE AWAY

A gift tag to attach to a gift, to be given to someone during the week.

4th Week of Advent

Listen to God-Bearers

BRING

Feedback from the experience of taking a gift to someone during the week.

An Advent wreath with four purple or red candles and a white candle in the middle, to represent Jesus' birth.

ICEBREAKER

Each person asks several others: 'Did last week's gift tag get used? What happened when you gave a gift – or is it private?'

CANDLE LIGHTING

Dim the lights

Leader In the wasteland may the Glory shine.
In the land of the lost may the King make his home.

Light one coloured candle

First All-knowing God, parents-in-God picture and pattern your ways.

All Forgive us for following idols and illusions.

Light a second coloured candle

Second All-seeing God, prophets shine like candles in the night.

All Forgive us for staying in the dark.

Light a third coloured candle

Third All-holy God, forerunners like John clear obstacles from your path.

All	Forgive us for blocking your way.
	Light the fourth coloured candle
Fourth	All-giving God, people like Mary offered their all as bearers of your Life.
All	Help us to be bearers of your life.

MUSIC

Listen to meditative music, such as from Margaret Rizza's CD.

GROUPS

'The Magnificat', is a well-known name for Mary's song which begins 'I magnify . . .'

In the light of this, discuss, in groups of four or five, the following statement: 'In our society we magnify what is unimportant and minimise what is truly important.'

BIBLE READING

Mary was willing to bear God's life, even though she could not understand how it could be or what it would mean. Mary's child was unique, but the abandonment of one's body and soul to be a bearer of God's life is not unique to Mary. In fact, the experience of Hannah, the barren wife who gave birth to the prophet Samuel, must have been much in Mary's thoughts. For Mary's prayer song draws inspiration from Hannah's. As excerpts from the two prayer songs are read, see if you can spot some similarities.

1st Reader   Luke 1:46-56
2nd Reader   1 Samuel 2:4-8

What similarities can you spot?

MEDITATION

There are many examples of people outside Bible lands who were God-bearers. Ireland's saint Brigid was known as 'Mary of the

Gael' ('the people's Mary'); in popular prayer visualisation she was the midwife at Christ's birth. This image reflected the fact that she was a 'midwife of faith for the Irish people'. Often a person, male or female, can be 'pregnant' with something God wants to bring to birth, big or small.

Advent invites us to participate in a process of transformation, which Jesus has begun in the human race. Jesus is: within us, unfolding, far from fully realised. In the silence, as you relax and focus on your breathing, ask: 'What seed has God put within my soul? What am I carrying that might be from God? With what am I pregnant?'

You may realise that you are too overwhelmed with other things to know the answer to these questions. Do not worry. God knows. Give those things to God, as Mary must have given to God her worries that her fiancé and her family would reject her, and that she would not be able to cope.

Have a few minutes of silence

DEVOTION

Leader Son of the prophets, on our longings

All Let your light shine.

Leader Son of Mary, on our littleness

All Let your light shine

Leader Son of Eternity, on our lying down

All Let your light shine.

Leader What gift of the Spirit was Mary given,
and what gifts does God want to give us?

First The gift of receiving – receiving all
manifestations of new life that the Great
Birther wishes to give. Only those who are
pure through and through can be such receivers.

Second The gift of bearing. Love bears all things. Only
those who love can be bearers.

Third   The gift of accompanying, and being fully present to others. Only those who are freed from self-concern can be accompaniers.

Fourth   The gift of tending, to practical and to deepest needs, without ever possessing. Only those who are secure in God can be tenders.

All   I give you assent with all my being.
I give you affection with all my senses.
I give you worship with all my mind.
I give you joy with all my frame.
I bow my knees before you.
I still my heart before you.
I am yours, and I will be yours,
every day of my life.

There may be a time of worship, prayer and sharing, according to the ethos of the group. All may sing the following to the tune of 'Amazing Grace':

Magnificat, magnificat,
magnificat, praise God!
Magnificat, magnificat,
magnificat, praise God.

All nations now will share my joy,
your gifts you have outpoured.
Your little ones you have made great;
I magnify the Lord.

Magnificat, magnificat,
praise God my soul, praise God!
The proud are downed, the poor raised up,
magnificat, praise God.

You fill the hungry with good things,
the rich you send away.
The promise made to Abraham
you ripen every day.

Magnificat, magnificat,
magnificat, praise God!
Magnificat, magnificat,
magnificat, praise God.

TAKE AWAY

Hold in your heart, each day and night of this week, anything God
has revealed to you or that is stirring in you.

P.S.
Celebrate!

LET DREAMS COME TRUE.

USE THE INSPIRATIONS TO HAVE

A TRULY GREAT CHRISTMAS.

The Community of Aidan and Hilda

The Community of Aidan and Hilda is a dispersed body of Christians who seek to cradle contemporary expressions of Christian spirituality and church, and to heal wounded lands. In the earthing of that commitment members draw inspiration from Celtic saints such as Aidan and Hilda.

Members follow a way of life, with a soul-friend, based on a rhythm of prayer, work, re-creation, study and outreach. They seek to weave together the separated strands of Christianity.

The Community has members and groups in four continents and advisers from different Church streams. In the UK it is an Associate Body of Churches Together in Britain and Ireland.

Its UK office and retreat house is The Open Gate, The Holy Island of Lindisfarne, Berwick-upon-Tweed TD15 2SD; aidan@theopengate.ndo.co.uk

Its website is: www.aidan.org.uk.

The story of the Community and a commentary on its Way of Life is published by Kevin Mayhew Ltd as *A Pilgrim Way*.